THE STORY OF LORD CLIVE

BY JOHN LANG
PICTURES BY STEWART ORR

Sandycroft Publishing

THE STORY OF LORD CLIVE

BY JOHN LANG

PICTURES BY STEWART ORR

First published 1906

This edition 2017

Sandycroft Publishing

http://sandycroftpublishing.com

TO
ST. CLAIR CUNNINGHAM

DEAR ST. CLAIR,

They tell me that you are going to be a soldier. I do not know upon which branch of the Service you have set your heart, but, whichever it may be, you cannot go far wrong if you take for your model that great fighter, Lord Clive, of some of whose deeds I have tried to tell you.

                Yours always,

                        JOHN LANG

CONTENTS

CHAPTER I: CLIVE'S BOYHOOD..1
CHAPTER II: CLIVE GOES TO INDIA..5
CHAPTER III: THE SIEGE OF ARCOT..15
CHAPTER IV: KAVERIPAK AND SAMIAVERAM....................21
CHAPTER V: THE BLACK HOLE OF CALCUTTA....................30
CHAPTER VI: THE BATTLE OF PLASSEY................................38
CHAPTER VII: DEATH OF SURAJAH DOWLAH—DEFEAT
    OF THE DUTCH—CLIVE'S END..49

LIST OF PICTURES

There he sat, perfectly happy and fearless..3
To Clive was given the command of the storming party...............13
Attacking the French guns at Kaveripak....................................23
An Irish deserter fired at Clive's head..26
"Water! Water!" the poor prisoners gasped................................34
Clive on the roof, watching the Battle of Plassey........................45
The Duke of Dorset fighting the Dutch fleet in the Hoogly.........52
One of the worst things Clive had to handle was a mutiny
    amongst the officers..54

CHAPTER I
CLIVE'S BOYHOOD

You have heard of India, of its riches and its grandeur and its glory, of its hundreds of millions of people, and of the great deeds that have been done there. But perhaps you have never heard who it was that gave India to England; you may possibly know nothing of Robert Clive, the boy who, when he was really little more than a boy, laid for us the foundations of the vast Empire in the East over which King Edward VII now reigns.

Clive was born on 29th September 1725, near Market, Drayton in Shropshire, where his people had owned an estate ever since about the time when Henry the First was King of England, which is a very long time indeed.

Even as a very small boy, Robert Clive was not quite like other boys of his age. Nothing could frighten him. He was like the boy in the fairy-tale who "did not know how to shiver," and he was so entirely without fear that sometimes his mother thought that her son was not quite sound in his mind, and even his father and his uncles were sometimes uneasy about him. At seven years old he was very much like that Scotch terrier whose solemn look was only to be accounted for (so his master said) by the fact that he "couldna get enough o' fighting." Clive was always fighting; he would fight anything and anybody, and he never gave in, nor knew when he was beaten. If a boy was too strong for him, Clive would fight again and again till he won. That is, of course, what every boy should do, but we don't all do it.

Clive (like a good many other boys, perhaps) would never learn his lessons, no matter how much he might be flogged—and a flogging, in those days was not a thing to laugh at. He was sent from school to school, but everywhere there was the same story: he was idle and bad, they said,—"a dunce" was the least ill name that was given to him. Of all his school-masters there was but one who saw in him any good, only one who said, "This boy may yet become a great man."

Clive's father is said to have been a man of violent temper, and perhaps it may have been because the father found the son difficult to manage that the little boy was sent away from home when he was only three years old. Whatever the reason, he was sent to Manchester, to the house of a Mr. Bayley, who had married his mother's sister. There Clive stopped for some years, and then, while still a very small boy, he went to a private school at Lostocke in Cheshire.

From Lostocke, when he was eleven, he was sent to Mr. Burslem's school at Market Drayton, and the people of that town: talked of "Bob" Clive's doings for many a long year afterwards. In all mischief he was first; wherever it was possible to get into a scrape, Bob Clive got into it. In the town, amongst the tradesmen, his hand was against every man, and every man's hand against him.

There was in Market Drayton a little band of boys of whom Clive was leader. Without cease they warred against the shopkeepers of the town, keeping the whole place in hot water. The band was really a little band of brigands, who made themselves to everyone a nuisance and a terror, and everywhere levied "blackmail." That is to say, if the band took a dislike to any tradesman, Clive, as leader, would go to that tradesman and say to him: "Now, if you do not pay us so much"—perhaps it might be money, or perhaps something else that the boys had set their hearts on—"we'll see that you have no peace; and there's no saying what may happen to your shop windows."

Generally the shopkeepers paid up, for they knew that Clive might be trusted to do what he said he would do. They had tried being defiant, but it did not pay. Once a tradesman had refused what was demanded, and the band had straightway, during heavy rain, built a dam in the gutter near his shop, so that the flood-water swamped the place and his goods were damaged. And when, before the water poured into the shop, the dam had burst at a weak spot, Clive threw himself into the breach, and with his body kept the water from escaping until the other boys repaired the dam. The shopkeeper, in self-defence, was forced to pay what the boys asked.

Nowadays such pranks could not be played, in a town, but at that time, you see, there were no regular police, and what was called the "Watch" was formed of feeble old men who were no match for mischievous boys. They were not very much good for anything, those old men, except to toddle about of nights, with a lantern, calling the hour.

Chapter I: Clive's Boyhood

There he sat, perfectly happy and fearless.

"Two o' clo-o-ck; and a fine frosty morning," perhaps they would shout in a long-drawn wail, at that hour. It is not easy to see of what particular use they were, except perhaps to make people, snug in bed, turn over sleepily and draw the blankets more snugly about their ears; just as the mate of a sailing-ship sometimes, when in port, orders a middy to call him at eight bells in the morning watch (the mate's usual time for going on duty when at sea), so that he may have the pleasure of turning round and dropping off asleep again.

But it was not only in mischief that Clive was leader. In everything where pluck was needed he was always first, and he never seemed to see danger, nor to shrink from risks that others dared not face. The greater the danger, during all his life the greater was his coolness.

There is at Market Drayton a church with a lofty tower, eighty feet or more in height. Near the top there are stone gargoyles (old-fashioned projecting waterspouts), shaped like a dragon's head and neck. Up to one of these Clive climbed at the risk of his life, and there, astride of a gargoyle, he sat, perfectly happy and fearless, with nothing to hold on by but the stone spout, whilst his boy friends and the townspeople stood shivering, each second expecting to see him lose his balance and come crashing on to the stones below.

It was a dangerous climb to get up; but it is always easier to climb up than it is to climb down. When you climb down you must look down, in order to see where your feet are to go, and to look down causes most people to become dizzy. Then people lose their heads, and sometimes can go no farther, either up or down. They clutch tightly till their hands become cramped, and then, if no help is possible, their grip loosens and they fall.

How Clive got safely to the ground is a mystery; the slightest mistake meant death. What he went up for is also a mystery. Old books say that it was "to get a smooth stone which lay on the projecting spout, for the pleasure of jerking it." But it is not easy to see how the "smooth stone" got on to the spout, nor, if it were there, how it could be seen from the ground. It seems much more likely that Clive climbed up to get a jackdaw's nest from some part of the tower.

CHAPTER II
CLIVE GOES TO INDIA

After a few years at Market Drayton, Clive was sent to a public school—Merchant Taylors'; but after a very brief stay he went to a private school in Hertfordshire, where, he remained till 1743.

In that year there came a big change in his life. His father got for him the appointment of what was called a writer in the East India Company's service, and Clive eagerly accepted it. Probably it seemed to him to be a great appointment, bringing with it endless possibilities. But had he guessed the truth, had he known what going to India, as a writer meant in those days, and how humdrum his life there was likely to be, it is possible that he would have been no more anxious to go than he had been to work, as his father wanted him to do, in a lawyer's office at home. He thought, probably, that he was going out to a life in which there might come plenty of fighting and never-ending possibilities of excitement and adventure. He did not know that to be a writer in the East India Company's service meant simply to be a clerk in a merchant's office, to sit all day at a desk adding up columns of dry figures, and doing other like drudgery.

The East India Company then was but a company of traders, holding no land in India beyond the small patches where were their trading stations, and for them paying rent to the native rajahs (or princes), who, in their turn, undertook the protection of the stations. Soldiers the company then had but few, and these mostly ill armed and not very well disciplined natives.

Such a life as was then possible for an Englishman in India was the last that was likely to suit Clive. The pay, too, was very poor, and though men sometimes made fortunes in India, it was only after years of hard drudgery; and generally, when they did make a fortune, in the making of it they lost their health.

From the very start Clive hated the life. There was no Suez Canal in those days; no great mail-steamers ploughed steadily along at seventeen or eighteen knots an hour, to land their passengers at

Bombay or Calcutta before a month has passed. A voyage to India in the middle of the eighteenth century was not a thing to be lightly undertaken. And so Clive learned.

He sailed from England early in the year 1743, and he did not reach Madras till near the end of 1744. The ship fell in with bad weather and had to put into Rio de Janeiro for repairs. There she lay for nine months. Then she lay at anchor at the Cape of Good Hope for another long spell; and so, when at last Clive landed at Madras, he had no money left, and he was obliged to borrow from the captain of the ship, who charged him very heavy interest for the loan.

Nor did Clive's bad luck end here. The friend to whom he had brought letters of introduction had left India and had gone home. Thus Clive was utterly "on his beam-ends." He was desperately homesick; he was short of money; the work of a clerk was hateful to him; he did not like his fellow-clerks, and kept apart from them. Thus he was not only without money, but without friends. There never was a less promising start of a great career.

Clive's first few months in India were wretched—so wretched, indeed, that it is said the poor boy, weary of his poverty and the dull grind of life, tried to commit suicide. It is told how one day an acquaintance happened to come into the room where Clive sat, miserable and alone, a loaded pistol lying by his side on the table.

"Will you fire that pistol out of the window?" asked Clive.

His companion took it up and pulled the trigger. Bang! went the pistol, filling the room with smoke.

"Surely," cried Clive, starting up with white face, "I must be meant for something great in this life! I have twice snapped that pistol at my head today, and each time it has missed fire."

After this Clive began to make a few friends, and to keep less to himself; but even then he did not cease to be homesick, nor, to repent of having chosen such a profession. "I have not enjoyed a happy day since I left my native land," he wrote to a cousin; and all his letters home were full of misery. About this time, however, the Governor of Madras took pity on him and gave him the run of his library; and thus Cline's days became less gloomy, for he was fond of reading, and made good use of the Governor's permission.

But the time had not yet come when events were to give Clive his opportunity, and to show of what stuff the lad was made. You must know that in those old days the French were our great trading rivals in India. As early as the year 1625 the English had made a settlement at a place thirty-six miles to the south of what is how Madras, and seven years later they had got from a native rajah, a grant of a small piece of land, on which they had built a fort for the protection of their storehouses. This place was named Madras, and the fort they called Fort St. George.

Both town and fort were very small, the latter not worthy of the name—having, indeed, no greater strength than a mud wall, protected by four small batteries, could give, and without outworks of any kind. It was not a place capable of much defense, even had there been troops enough to defend it. But in 1744 the whole English population did not exceed three hundred souls. Of these, perhaps two hundred were soldiers, but very few of them had ever "smelt powder."

Down the coast, less than one hundred miles south from Madras, there was in those days a French Settlement at a place known as Puducheri, a name which in time became changed to Pondicherry, by which it is still known. The place remains to this day a French colony.

Naturally, when in 1745 the news reached India that war had been declared between England and France, the settlers in the English and French colonies expected soon to be at each other's throats. But the Governor of Pondicherry, acting on orders from Paris, wrote to the Governor of Madras suggesting that the war in Europe should not be allowed to extend to these colonies. The Governor of Madras, however, had received orders to a different effect from London. He was told that an English squadron was on its way to Madras and would shortly arrive, and that this squadron was meant to be used for the purpose of destroying the French settlements and all their shipping. The Governor of Madras, therefore, was unable to agree to the proposal of the French Governor.

Thereupon M. Dupleix, the French Governor, sent a message to the native prince from whom both English and French rented the land on which their settlements stood, asking him for help, or at least that he would prevent the English from attacking the French at Pondicherry. This prince, who was called the Nawab of the Karnatic, had never seen the English fight, and he had, indeed, a very poor opinion of all Europeans as fighting-men. He sent word to Mr. Morse, the Governor of Madras, telling him that he (the Nawab) would not allow any fighting between the English and the French, and Mr. Morse thought it well to obey this order. For a time, therefore, there was peace between the two colonies, though the English squadron which had been sent out had captured a great many French vessels.

But in June 1746, Commodore Peyton, who was then in command of the squadron, heard that some French men-of-war had been seen cruising off the coast of Ceylon, which was then a Dutch colony. He accordingly sailed south, and on 6th July met the French squadron. A battle raged all that afternoon and part of the next day, when Peyton, finding that one of his largest ships was badly damaged, made sail, and left to the French squadron all the honour of the fight. It was not a very glorious action for us.

On 8th July the French vessels anchored off Pondicherry, and the admiral of the fleet and the Governor of Pondicherry resolved; now to attack Madras. Accordingly, on 15th September, the Frenchmen, under Admiral La Bourdonnais, arrived off Fort St. George, landed 1100 European troops and some sipahis (or sepoys, as we now call them), and demanded that the place should be surrendered.

Mr. Morse, the Governor, had also (as well as M. Dupleix) applied to the Nawab for help. But, with his request he had not sent the present which an Indian prince always expected to receive when a favour was begged from him, and therefore the Nawab gave no reply to the English. As Mr. Morse had no troops with which to fight the French force, he was therefore obliged to surrender, and on 21st September it was agreed that the town and fort should be given up, and that the English garrison and all the English in the town should be prisoners of war.

Thus Clive became a prisoner in the hands of the French.

And now things began to take shape in the way which gave him his opportunity. Such were the beginnings from which Clive started his wonderful career.

When the Nawab heard of the taking of Madras by the French, he sent to M. Dupleix a message ordering him to give up the place. But Dupleix put off from day to day, and finally, the Nawab, seeing that the French had no intention of obeying his orders, sent an army of 10,000 men to turn them out.

Meantime a tremendous storm had driven the French fleet away from the coast of India, and Dupleix was thus left with only a few hundred French troops and 700 sepoys. The leader of the Nawab's army, fancying that his task was a very simple one, attacked the French at the village of St. Thomé, but, after a tremendous fight, the better discipline of the French troops defeated the native army with great slaughter.

This was the first time that a European force had fought against a native army, and the result caused M. Dupleix to fancy that henceforward he had nothing to fear in India. He had beaten the English, and now he had defeated the Nawab. Vaingloriously, he despised both.

On 9th November the commander of the French troops, Colonel Paradis, entered Madras. Upsetting the arrangements which had been already made by Admiral La Bourdonnais, he ordered all the English who should refuse to take an oath of allegiance to the French Governor, to leave the town within four days.

The English officials to be removed to Pondicherry as prisoners on parole. That is to say, they were to stay in Pondicherry and to give their word of honour never again during the war to fight against, or to take any part against, the French, or to help their own side. But many of the English refused to give this parole, and several of them escaped and made their way to Fort St. David, a small place about sixteen miles south of Pondicherry, which had been bought by the English in 1691.

Clive was one of those who refused to give his parole.

Disguised as natives, he and a friend escaped, and hardly had they arrived at Fort St. David when fighting began there. The French were determined to turn the English out of India, and they laid siege to the place, trying again and again to take it by assault. But assault after assault failed, and each time that the French were beaten back, Clive's dash and bravery were noticed by everybody. Now he was in his element; this was a man's game, he felt, and at last he was free from the hated desk and the detested columns of figures. Life was worth living.

But his whole time was not taken up in fighting the French. One evening during the siege, Clive was playing at cards after dinner, and he was losing steadily. Presently something occurred which made him very carefully watch the play, and very soon he saw without any possibility of doubt that his opponent, an officer, was, cheating. Clive threw down his cards, and told him that he declined to play longer or to pay the money he had lost.

"Do you accuse me of cheating, sir?" roared the officer, starting; up in a fury. "Yes, I do," said Clive. "You shall very humbly apologise to me for that insult, sir; or you shall fight me."

"Very well," said Clive, "I will fight you. I refuse to apologize. You *did* cheat."

Pistols were got, and the two went out, without seconds, to fight. Seconds were friends who were usually taken, to load the pistols, and to see that the fighting was quite fair and that neither of the fighters fired before the signal was given. It was very unusual for a fight to take place without someone to see fair play.

Duels with pistols were fought in several different ways.

Sometimes the fighters stood twelve paces apart, and fired when the word was given. Sometimes they stood back to back, and, at the word "march," walked twelve yards away from each other, firing as soon as they could turn round after reaching the twelfth step.

And sometimes only one of two pistols was loaded, and the fighters, separated only by the width of a handkerchief, drew lots for choice of pistols and for first shot, neither knowing, of course, which was the loaded pistol. Then the man who had drawn the right to shoot first, fired, and if he had had the luck also to choose the loaded pistol, his opponent was as good as a dead man. But if, on the other hand, the first man had not happened to choose the loaded pistol, then he, in his turn, was certain to die.

It was uncommonly like cold-blooded murder, but it had this advantage, that it gave a man who was a bad shot an equal chance with the man who was a good one, and it sometimes made a bully think twice before he challenged anybody, because the challenged man had the right to say how he would fight.

There were many men in those bad old days who were such practised shots that if a glove were thrown up in the air, they could put a bullet through the thumb of the glove before it reached the ground. Such men were almost certain to kill their adversary in a duel, and they were forever picking quarrels with, and shooting, poor wretches who had no chance to stand up to them. There is no dueling now, happily, except in France, where they don't often do each other any harm, and in Germany, where the students slice each other's faces, and swagger about, showing their scars.

Clive and his opponent fought at twelve paces, and there being no seconds, one of themselves gave the signal, "Are you ready?

"Fire!" Clive's pistol went off first. He missed.

"Now, sir," said his adversary, who had not fired, marching quickly up, and putting his pistol to Clive's head, "beg for your life."

"Very well," answered Clive, "I ask you for my life."

"Now, withdraw your charge of cheating, and make me a most humble apology."

"I refuse to do anything of the kind," said Clive.

"I'll blow your brains out where you stand, unless you apologise at once. Quick!" cried the officer, pressing the cold muzzle of his pistol to Clive's forehead.

"Fire away!" said Clive coolly. "I said you cheated, and I say so still. You did cheat, and I refuse to pay."

His enemy looked at him steadily for a minute, uncertain what to do or say. Then flinging away his pistol, he left the ground, muttering, "The boy is mad."

Clive afterwards always refused to give any account of this card party. "No," he said, "the man has given me my life, and though I will not pay him money which was not fairly won, and will not again be friendly with him, yet I will never do him an injury."

On another occasion during the siege, someone accused Clive of having "shown the white feather." Ammunition was badly wanted for the battery of which Clive was in command, and, in his hurry, instead of sending a corporal or sergeant, Clive himself ran for it.

An officer in another battery, seeing him running towards the rear, said that Clive went himself in order to get out of danger. Clive was furious, and demanded that the officer should apologise. This was refused, whereupon Clive challenged the man. As they were retiring to a quiet place to fight, the officer turned and struck Clive, who at once drew his sword, and was with difficulty prevented from killing him. A court of inquiry was at once held, and the officer who had accused Clive of being a coward was ordered to beg his pardon in front of the whole battalion. But this did not satisfy Clive. The man must also fight him, he said. The officer, however, refused to fight, whereupon Clive, waving his cane over the wretched man's head, said—

"You are too great a coward for me to thrash as you deserve. You cur!"

The man resigned his commission next day, and left the army.

Many assaults on Fort St. David had now been made, and after the failure of the fourth assault the tables were turned on the French. Instead of being the besiegers they became the besieged.

An English squadron arrived on the coast, and later, a fleet under Admiral Boscawen brought troops. The French retired to Pondicherry, and the English laid siege to it. But they in their turn were beaten back, in spite of much brave fighting, in which Clive always greatly distinguished himself. Finally, after a siege lasting two months, the English retired to Fort St. David, having lost over a thousand men by wounds and through sickness. But before the French could again attack that place, news arrived of the signing of peace by England and France at Aix-la-Chapelle. By this Treaty of Peace the French were obliged to hand back Madras to the English, which they did with very ill grace, leaving the place in bad condition, and with most of the fortifications rendered useless.

But, though there was for a time no fighting in Europe between the two nations, there was far from being peace between them in India. M. Dupleix found that he still had something to fear there.

The native princes who had helped the French against the English continued their warfare against the Indian allies of England. Thus both nations were obliged to help those who already had helped them. The Rajah of Tanjore, whose throne during the fighting had been taken from him, was one of the allies of the English, and the Governor of Fort St. David now sent a force of 430 Europeans and 1000 sepoys to help him to recover his throne. At least that was the reason given out; but the truth probably was that the English wanted to have for themselves the Fort of Devikota, which stands on the sea at the mouth of the River Coleroon, and this seemed a good chance to get possession of it.

Clive went with the force as a volunteer. The expedition failed, partly because the officer in command, Captain Cope, was no great soldier, and partly because the ex-Rajah had amongst the natives few friends who would give him help. The season too was against it; the heavy rains of the monsoon had begun, when marching is almost impossible.

But another attempt was soon made under the command of the distinguished Major Lawrence. This time Clive was given a temporary commission as lieutenant; he was not yet a regular soldier. The force went by sea to Devikota, and after four days battering at the walls with cannon, a breach was made through which Major Lawrence

To Clive was given the command of the storming party.

thought it possible to enter the fort. To Clive was given the command of the storming party, a great honour, and one after Clive's own heart.

As the storming party made its rush for the breach in the wall, the enemy's cavalry charged. Of twenty-nine Europeans in the party, twenty-six fell, fighting bravely. Clive and two others managed to reach Lawrence, who was bringing up the main body of the troops, and though the cavalry again charged fiercely, this time they were driven back with heavy loss, and Devikota was taken. Lawrence said of Clive at this time that he was "a brave soldier," whose "presence of mind never left him in the greatest danger," and that, "he led an army like an experienced officer and a brave soldier." Such praise must have made Clive feel very proud, for he had had no training as a soldier, and he was little more than a boy.

After taking Devikota, the troops returned to Fort St. David. Here the learned that during their absence a revolution had taken place in the part of India called Karnatic, which lies inland from the Madras coast, and that several native princes were at war with each other. Two of these, Muzaffar Jang and Chunda Sahib, were supported by the French. Another of the princes who wanted to claim the throne of the Karnatic for himself, was defeated and slain in battle by Muzaffar and Chundra Sahib. The English supported the claims of Muhammad Ali, a son of this slain prince, who, after the battle in which his father was killed, had fled to Trichinopoli.

Now, Muzaffar and Chunda Sahib and the French decided to march against Trichinopoli, and to capture Muhammad Ali; but the hesitated to do so as long as the English fleet remained on the coast. The fleet, however, through a mistake of the English Governor, was allowed to sail, whereupon the two princes and their French allies at once marched against Trichinopoli. The general result of events was such that the French became, for the time, a much greater power in Southern India than were the English. "And so," as Colonel Malleson writes, "and so, but for one man, it would have remained." That one man was Clive.

CHAPTER III
THE SIEGE OF ARCOT

After his return from Devikota, Clive was made commissary of the forces, but before he could take up his duties, he fell ill and was sent for a long cruise in the Bay of Bengal. On his return in 1751 he fitted out a small force for the relief of Trichinopoli, which the French and their allies were still trying to take. Then, as commissary, he accompanied another body of English and native troops which had been ordered to march to a place called Volkonda, about forty miles north east of Trichinopoli, there to try French army which was marching against Trichinopoli. But the officer in command of the force with which Clive went was not a very clever soldier, and he greatly mismanaged the expedition. Clive could see, but he could not prevent, the commanding officer's mistakes, so he left him and returned to Fort St. David.

There he found that an expedition, made up of eighty Europeans and three hundred sepoys, was about to start to convoy provisions to Trichinopoli. But the Governor had no officer whom he thought fit to take the command, so he had appointed a Mr. Pigot, a civilian, to lead it. Clive volunteered to go with him, and in three days they had carried the expedition to a spot beyond which there was no danger of its being captured.

Mr. Pigot and Clive then turned back for Fort St. David, through a country which was swarming with the enemy's cavalry. Again and again, as they pushed their cautious way by jungle paths and byways, bodies of horsemen dashed at the two Englishmen, trying to capture or to kill them. Again and again would Clive and Pigot turn on their enemies and charge, or, if needs must, gallop for their lives. And at last they reached Fort St. David in safety.

At Fort St. David they found another expedition about to set out; but again the Governor had no officer fit to lead it. Clive, of course, was only a civilian; though he had fought at Pondicherry and at Fort St. David, and at Devikota, his commission had only been what is called a temporary one, that is to say, it was meant to last only during the one campaign. Now he decided that he would remain a civilian no longer, and he applied to the Governor for a commission in the army, offering, if necessary, to join without pay.

The Governor thought so highly of Clive that he gave him a commission as captain, and ordered him to march at once, with the few troops available, to Devikota, there to join another small force, and to proceed to Trichinopoli, whence he was to report to the Governor the state of affairs.

At Trichinopoli, Clive found Chunda Sahib with a huge host of native troops and 900 Frenchmen, besieging Muhammad Ali in the fortress. Muhammad Ali had but 5000 of his own men and 600 English soldiers, and in the whole force there was scarcely an officer or man who was not out of spirits, and who did not feel certain that nothing was to be expected but defeat. There was no money to pay the native troops; the English soldiers had lost faith in their officers, and most of the officers had lost faith in themselves. Affairs were about as bad as bad could be.

Clive saw that something must be done at once to rouse both officers and men; they could not fight if they went into battle believing that they must be beaten. Now Clive had always been fond of reading books about great soldiers, and he cast about in his mind for what some of these great commanders would have done in like case. He knew that Chunda Sahib, keen to take Trichinopoli, had brought all his best soldiers there, and had left his capital, Arcot, without any good troops. Here, Clive saw, was his chance. He set off at once to Fort St. David, and laid before Mr. Saunders, the Governor, his idea of taking Arcot. Mr. Saunders saw at once that if Arcot were taken, Chunda Sahib would be obliged to withdraw his men from before Trichinopoli in order to try to get back Arcot.

The Governor was not afraid of taking responsibility. There were at Madras and at Fort St. David only 350 European soldiers in all, but he promised 200 of them for the expedition, and to Clive he gave the command, Clive, who had been a soldier for just one month.

"It was on the 26th of August 1751 that Clive set forth from Madras on the march that was to bring him immortal fame, and to secure for his countrymen the first footing on the ladder which was to conduct them to Empire."

Clive had with him in his little army but 200 English soldiers, 300 sepoys, and three guns. There were in all but eight officers, six of whom had never been under fire, and the troops themselves were without experience of warfare. It was not a force from which at best much could be expected; it was a force which, badly led, could meet only with disaster. But the brilliant genius of Clive brought it through with extraordinary success.

In three days the little army was within twenty-seven miles of Arcot. Clive learned that there were 1200 native soldiers in the place, but that their discipline was not good, and he thought that it might be taken by surprise.

At once, in the middle of a terrible storm of rain, he set off with all possible speed, and two days later he "rushed" the town and fort without losing a man. Then he marched against the Fort of Timeri, where the garrison of 600 native soldiers fled without fighting. Clive thereupon went back to Ascot, but two days later, hearing that 2000 of the enemy had returned to Timeri, he marched out and gave them a severe beating; but because he had no heavy guns with which to pound the mud walls, he was not able to take the fort.

Now Clive with all his might set about collecting provisions and making the walls and fortifications of Arcot as strong as possible, for well he knew that soon he must be attacked by the French and by thousands of natives.

He wrote to Madras for some eighteen-pounder guns, which were at once sent. But the enemy had heard of their despatch, and they determined that the guns should never reach Arcot. Clive, through his spies hearing of the enemy's plans, left only eighty men in Arcot (thirty English soldiers and fifty natives), and marched hastily to save the guns.

Meantime, whilst Clive was absent on this expedition, the enemy made a fierce attack on Arcot, thinking to sweep away with ease the few English soldiers left there. But the brave little garrison held its own, every man fighting like a hero, and when Clive returned in safety with the guns, Chunda Sahib's men retreated.

Now began the famous siege of Arcot. Even after all Clive's work, the place hardly seemed one that could possibly be defended, against such a force as was being sent against it. The walls were in many parts broken and in ruins; the ditches were almost without water; there was little shelter for the troops whilst they fought, and it was found impossible to mount guns on the narrow ramparts. Moreover, sickness and wounds had brought the garrison down to

120 Englishmen and 200 sepoys, with, in all, but four officers. What were they, to meet the many thousands that Chunda Sahib and the French could, hurl against them?

The eyes of all India were eagerly watching what was going on at Arcot, and many native princes, struck with wonder at what Clive had already done, and impressed by the fighting powers of the English, now sent troops to help the Prince Muhammad Ali, whom the English were supporting. The whole future of England and France in India depended on whether or not Clive could hold out in Arcot.

On 23rd September Chunda Sahib's hordes of warriors, strengthened by French troops, closed round the city. Day and night, for fifty days there was no cease in their assaults, no rest for the little garrison. Clive was everywhere; wherever danger was greatest, where the storm of bullets fell thickest, where the fight was fiercest, there he was to be found, and wherever he went came victory. Fired by his example, his men fought with a furious energy against which nothing could stand, and the sepoys now, for the first time, showed those qualities of which they have so many times since given proof, a courage and a self-denial, a capacity to endure fatigue and to withstand hunger and thirst, that are worthy of the best soldiers in the world.

Provisions were scarce, and the sepoys came to Clive, and said that the English men needed food more than they did, and that if all the rice were given to the English, they themselves could live and fight on the gruel-like mess which was left after the rice was boiled.

The supply of water began to run out, and enough could only be got with great difficulty and danger. Fighting is at best a thirsty business, and when men fight under the scorching sun of India, thirst becomes an agony. Yet those brave sepoys, when water was brought to the sore-pressed garrison, stood back and refused to drink till the Englishmen had drunk their fill.

Nothing was left undone by the enemy in their efforts to take Arcot. A great bribe of money and jewels was even offered to Clive if he would but surrender. If he refused, they said, the fort would be at once stormed, and every man in it would be slaughtered without mercy. But Clive only answered that they had better think twice before they dared to come within reach of Englishmen.

And now, at last, after seven weeks of never-ending cannon-fire, the enemy had battered a breach in the wall, a breach big enough for them to pour through in numbers. It was the day of a great Mahommedan festival, a day when, even to the present time, the Moslem inhabitants of India work themselves into a frenzy of religious enthusiasm. All good Mahommedans who during this festival fell fighting against Infidels,—(that is to say, Christians),— they believe will by such a death atone for all the sins committed during their lives, and will pass straightway to Heaven—to the Garden of the Houris.

It was on this day, then, that Chunda Sahib's commander ordered an assault to be made on Arcot. He was sure of success. But to make success doubly sure, he caused drugs to be served out to his troops, drugs which increased their frenzy to madness. Death was nothing to these men, they courted it. What was Death but Heaven, and forgiveness of all their sins? Who could stand against such men?

"Through the breach they rushed, sure of victory, for the defenders, too few in number at the beginning, had now lost very many men, and those that were left were worn and weak with hunger and want of sleep.

For an hour Clive and his men fought furiously, sometimes borne back, but never despairing. Muskets grew hot with firing, smoke and dust swirled in clouds round the fierce-eyed men who swayed and fought and panted for breath as the bayonets grew red, and the ground slippery, with blood.

Then, before men could realise what had happened, the long strain was over; the enemy were running for their lives, beaten and humiliated. Before daylight next morning they had disappeared.

The siege of Arcot was over, and the fame of the English, and especially of their leader, spread far and wide. In the eyes of the natives, Clive was the greatest man in India; through fire and water, to death, they would have followed him.

But Clive did not think that he had done enough. He was not content to have beaten the enemy; he must follow him up and strike blow on blow. Joined by 1000 Mahratta cavalry, he marched to attack, in his turn, the army which for so long a time had been attacking him, an army now strengthened by fresh French troops from Pondicherry. This army was far more than twice as strong as Clive's little force, and when its commander saw how few were Clive's men, he turned back, thinking to finally crush the English. But where Clive had halted there were in his front rice-fields, across which troops could only attack by marching along a narrow causeway; one of his flanks was protected by a village, the other by a grove of palm-trees, both places easy to hold.

The French soldiers tried to advance across the causeway, while their native cavalry in swarms attacked the village and the palm grove. Clive brought all his guns to bear on the causeway, and swept the Frenchmen off it, till they turned and fled. Then dashing at them with his English soldiers before the French could rally, he broke the enemy's centre, and the whole army fled, panic-stricken. Clive followed them up till dark, killing and slaying.

Then, leaving a garrison to hold Arcot, he returned, after some further successful fighting, to Madras. Here he laid before the Governor his plans for the future against the French and their allies. A new expedition, led by Clive, was to go to the relief of Trichinopoli as soon as fresh troops should arrive from Bengal.

CHAPTER IV
KAVERIPAK AND SAMIAVERAM

On February 22nd Clive marched at the head of 380 Englishmen, 1300 sepoys, and six field guns. His anxiety to reach Arcot again was great, because he had cause to believe that a French and native army meant to attack that place. After failing to find the enemy at two spots where his information told him that they had encamped, he was making for Arcot, pressing on by long forced marches. At sunset on the 23rd he was near to a place called Kaveripak. Though Clive did not know it, here lay the French, hidden from sight. They had laid a trap for Clive, who had no cavalry to act as scouts, and he had marched right into it!

The French position was very strong, and they had posted near the road along which the English were marching, but hidden from view, a battery of nine guns supported by some of their best men. In a dry watercourse near at hand they had posted nearly all their infantry, both French and native. Cavalry waited behind a grove of mango trees, ready to charge the English as soon as the guns had thrown them into disorder. Everything was ready; the trap was set, and the mouse had run into it.

The thunder of the guns on his right was the first notice Clive had that the French were near him. His own guns were in the rear, and before they could be brought up many of his men had fallen. The enemy's cavalry began to move out quickly to try to get behind him. It was a position of very great danger, and the English force would have been destroyed if their leader had lost his head. But Clive never lost his head; the greater the danger, the cooler he became; the worse fix he was in, the more cheerfully did he set about getting out of it. Now, with men every moment falling around him, he gave his orders as calmly as he might have done on parade; his confidence in himself was such that his men could not but believe that all was yet well.

But the chances were all against him; he could neither advance nor retreat: he must fight where he was. And the French had all the best of the position, besides having a stronger force of infantry, as well as 2500 cavalry, an arm of which Clive had none. He must fight, and he must win. If he lost, not only would his own army be destroyed, but Trichinopoli must fall, and then the French would be all-powerful in Southern India. What was to be done?

The firing had now been going on for more than four hours. It was dark, men were falling fast, and those remaining were beginning to be disheartened.

There was just a chance, Clive thought, that the grove where the French guns were posted might have been left unguarded In its rear. He selected a sergeant, and sent him with a few sepoys to try to find out the truth about that position, and soon the sergeant rejoined him to say that there were no French troops in the rear of the grove. Clive at once took 200 of his best Europeans—more than half of all he had left, for numbers had fallen—and 400 sepoys, and himself stealthily led them through the darkness towards the rear of the grove. But, before he could get half-way to the grove, he knew, from the lessening of the fire of the men whom he had left to hold his first position, that they were losing heart and were becoming panic-stricken, and he knew that soon they would turn and fly.

Hastily making over the command of the storming party to the next senior officer, Lieutenant Keene, he hurried back to his old position, barely in time to stop his men from running away, confused and disheartened. Clive's arrival gave them back their courage, but he knew that he could not again trust them alone; they fought on, but they could not do much more than hold their own even with him at their head. They had been shaken, and their panic might return.

Meantime, Lieutenant Keene had led his party to a spot three hundred yards behind the grove from which the French guns were pounding away. There he halted, and sent forward an officer who could speak French, to examine the position. This officer, Ensign Symmonds, hurried off, and very soon, in a dry watercourse, came on a large body of native soldiers who were chattering there. As soon as they saw Symmonds, they jumped up to shoot him, but Symmonds coolly shouted to them in French, and they, concluding that he must be a French officer, let him pass.

Symmonds went right on to the grove, where he saw the Frenchmen loading and firing their guns, whilst about a hundred infantry soldiers were so busy firing their muskets at Clive and his men that they never thought of looking to their rear. Symmonds

Chapter IV: Kaveripak and Samiaveram

Attacking the French guns at Kaveripak.

hurried back by another way, so as to avoid the native troops, and at once Keene marched his party, unseen, to within thirty yards of the French guns. Here they halted and poured in a volley.

The French were so astonished and taken by surprise that they never attempted to fire in return, but ran for their lives and crowded into an empty house, where Keene forced them to surrender and to give up their arms.

The battle was won, for the enemy, seeing the guns taken and the Frenchmen captured, ran in all directions.

Clive had not only taken nine guns and three mortars, and many prisoners, but he had shown the natives that the English were more than a match for the French. Hitherto the natives of India had believed that the French were much the better fighting-men. This new lesson they never forgot.

Clive's losses at Kaveripak were heavy, but not nearly so heavy as those of the French; and however many men he may have lost, he had at any rate saved Southern India.

He now hurried back to Fort St. David, whence he was on the point of starting once again, with an expedition to Trichinopoli, when Major Stringer Lawrence, his senior officer, arrived from England.

Lawrence, of course, at once took command, and his operations were very successful. He forced the French to fall back, and to take up a position on an island in a river. Then he sent Clive to the other side of the river, with 400 English troops, 700 sepoys, and some native cavalry, to try to cut the French line of communications, as it is called. That is to say — he was to try to get between the French and the place from which they got their supplies. This Clive did very successfully.

But whilst he was encamped one night at a place called Samiaveram, the French commander, thinking that the English had gone away, sent a force of eighty Europeans (half of whom, I am sorry to say, were deserters from the English), and 700 sepoys, to seize that place. Clive and his men, utterly worn out with marching and fighting, were sound asleep, and the sentries were not much more wide awake. Clive was lying in a house—a kind of inn; his English troops were sleeping in two pagodas which they were using as barracks, whilst the native soldiers lay about on the ground.

When the French force came near in the dark, an English sentry challenged. But one of the deserters, an Irishman, told the sentry that they had been sent by Major Lawrence to strengthen Clive, and the party was allowed to march on, guided by one of the garrison towards Clive's quarters.

When they reached the smaller of the two pagodas, the Frenchmen were again challenged, and this time they replied by firing a volley through the open doors of the pagoda on to the sleeping soldiers. Then they rushed to the door of the inn, where Clive and his officers slept, and poured in a fire there. Crash upon crash went the volleys; a sentry fell dead close to Clive, and a box at his feet was shattered to pieces.

Surely to be so awakened in the dark from a sound sleep was enough to confuse and to shake the nerve of even the bravest of men. But in one second Clive had all his wits about him. Jumping up, he ran to the largest of the two pagodas, in which were 200 of his men.

"Follow me, men!" he shouted, as he ran out of the building. Then halting, he formed his men alongside a regiment of sepoys who were loosing off volleys in every direction in the darkness.

Clive gave the order to these men to "Cease fire," but at once one of them made a savage cut at him with his "tulwar," wounding him in the shoulder. "Cease fire!" again shouted Clive. But the order was a useless one, for these men were French sepoys, and not Clive's men at all.

At this moment up came six Frenchmen. "Rendez-vous!" one of them shouted to Clive; "you are my prisoner."

"Prisoner!" said Clive. "It is you, and not I, who may talk of surrendering. Look around. You will see that you are surrounded."

The Frenchmen were scared, and ran off to tell their commanding officer. Clive then speedily rallied his men who were in the other pagoda, whereupon the French sepoys ran out of the place. Meantime the Frenchmen and the English deserters, seeing themselves, as they thought, in a trap, had run into the smaller of the two pagodas, which they held till daylight. Then, at an early hour in the morning, their commanding officer led them out into the open, where Clive's men received them with a volley which killed twelve of them, and the Frenchmen scurried back to the pagoda like rabbits to their holes.

Clive, not wishing to shed more blood than he could help, now came to the front, and, pointing out to them that brave men could do no more than they had already done, asked them to surrender. Instantly one of them, an Irish deserter, who stood close to him,

An Irish deserter fired at Clive's head.

Chapter IV: Kaveripak and Samiaveram

raised his musket and fired point blank at Clive's head. In some strange way the man missed his aim, (though at such a short distance it would seem almost impossible to miss), and the bullet went through the bodies of two sergeants who stood behind Clive, killing them both. The commander of the French, disgusted with the act of the Irishman, then surrendered with his whole force, and I have no doubt that the Irish deserter was hanged, as he deserved to be.

Clive sent his native cavalry to follow up the French sepoys who had fled during the night, and it was said that not a man of them was left alive. The cavalry hunted them far and near, and chased them into every corner. It was an ill day for the French sepoys.

After this, speedily came the end of the operations. On 15th May Clive took the town of Paichanda. Thus he forced the French commander, d'Auteuil, to retreat to Volkonda, where he was obliged to surrender. Three days later, another French officer, with all his men, gave himself up; and finally, the whole French force before Trichinopoli surrendered to Major Lawrence. Clive had thereafter some months of hard work but no great fighting, and when the campaign was over he returned to rest at Madras. Here he married Miss Maskeleyne, the sister of one of the few friends whom he had made while he was yet a writer in the East India Company's service.

But all Clive's fighting and campaigning had severely tried his health, and he became so ill that he was obliged to apply for leave to visit Europe. Before leaving, however, there was more work for him to do. Two forts between Madras and Pondicherry, Covelong and Chingleput, were still held by French garrisons. It was determined that these places must be taken.

But the only force that could then be spared for the work was not one that any officer would care to command. There were 200 English recruits who had only just arrived from home. Not only were they without any idea of discipline, but they were almost undrilled. They were the roughest of the rough, wretched creatures picked off the streets of London, small in size, weak in constitution, and ignorant of how to use a musket. With them were 500 newly enrolled sepoys, men unknown to their officers, and almost without knowledge of drill.

What a force with which to march again well-trained French soldiers! No officer but Clive would have thought even of the possibility of success.

But, ill as he was, he took command. It is said that when a shot from the Fort of Covelong killed one of these recruits, all the rest threw away their muskets and ran for their lives. It was only with much difficulty that Clive stopped and rallied them. On another occasion it is said that the noise of a gun so frightened a sentry that hours afterwards he was found hiding in a well. But Clive gradually taught this rabble that there was not so much danger from bullets as they supposed, that they need not necessarily be killed each time the enemy fired at them.

At last this extraordinary force succeeded in taking Covelong. Almost immediately afterwards Clive learned that a strong body of French troops, not knowing that Covelong had fallen, was marching from Chingleput to its relief. Clive hid his men in the jungle by the side of the road, and as the French soldiers came up, Clive's men fired, killing a hundred of the French. Then the English dashed out, took 300 prisoners, and chased the remainder to the gates of Chingleput, a very strong fortress, to which they now laid siege. In a day or two a breach was battered in the walls, and Clive was just on the point of giving orders to storm, when the French commander hoisted the white flag and surrendered.

Who but Clive could in so short a time have taught such men the art of war; who but he could have put into them the spirit of soldiers?

In February 1753 he sailed from Madras for England.

Only ten years had passed since he left his native land, but what a change these ten years had made in Clive! He had come out a boy, poor, unhappy, without prospects, and looked upon by his father and his friends as a boy little likely to succeed in life—thought, indeed, to be a "booby." He returned a young man, covered with glory, a hero in the eyes of the world, rich, and brilliantly successful.

What more perfect revenge could he have taken over those who had laughed at him and called him "dunce"! Even his father, who when he first heard that his son was beginning to make a name for himself; had said, "Well, the booby has some sense after all, I suppose," now joined the throng of his son's admirers, and thought that nothing could be too good for his boy. Truly, a wonderful homecoming was this, enough to turn the head of a weaker man.

The Court of Directors of the East India Company gave a great banquet in his honour, and voted him a diamond-hilted sword as a mark of their admiration. But Clive, ever generous, would only accept the sword on condition that a similar one was given to Major Lawrence.

Nor was it only in such acts that Clive's generosity showed itself. He was ever ready to help his friends, to share with his relations all that he possessed. He had brought home with him a considerable fortune, and one of his first acts was to pay all his father's debts, for the old gentleman had got into difficulties from which he could not free himself. Then Clive paid off a mortgage on the old family estate, and settled money on his sisters. His family had good reason indeed to welcome him home.

CHAPTER V
THE BLACK HOLE OF CALCUTTA

After a year in England, Clive stood for Parliament at the General Election, and was returned for the borough of St. Michael, in Cornwall. On petition, however, he was unseated. Election petitions in those days were not heard before judges, as is now the case, but were heard before a Committee of the House of Commons. The Committee decided in Clive's favour, but then the question came later before the whole House. It became, therefore, not a question as to whether Clive had or had not been properly returned, but a Party question, and that Party which Clive supported was not so strong as the other, and he thus lost his seat. The disappointment was a grievous one, and he determined to return to India.

Before sailing, he received a commission as lieutenant-colonel in the royal army. Up to this time he had held his commission only from the East India Company. He was also appointed Governor and Commander of Fort St. David, and was named as the future Governor of Madras.

He sailed for Bombay in 1755, taking with him three companies of artillery and 300 infantry. On arrival at Bombay, he employed his men in harrying the stronghold of Angria, a pirate chief, who had for years been a pest on that coast. No town was safe from him; no trading vessel could sail in those waters without almost the certainty of capture; no man's life was secure; on all the Malabar coast Angria was feared and hated. Now his end had come. Clive wiped him out, and destroyed his stronghold after two days' fighting, and plunder worth £150,000 was taken and divided amongst the troops and the fleet.

After this Clive sailed for Fort St. David, where he arrived on 20th June 1756. That is a day never to be forgotten in the history of India and of England; a day the horror of which yet lives, and men forget now, when they talk of "The Black Hole of Calcutta," that they speak of horrors which took place 50 years ago. Except in the punishment of the fiends who caused the awful torture and death of

Chapter V: The Black Hole of Calcutta

so many helpless white men, Clive had no part in the affair. But no story could be told of Clive's life without telling also of the tragedy of the Black Hole of Calcutta.

The Nawab Surajah Dowlah, native ruler of Bengal, a very young man, thoroughly vicious and bad, for reasons of his own had seized the English factory at Cossimbazar. After plundering it and putting the small garrison in prison, he had marched against Calcutta, where he believed that the English had vast treasure hidden away. Surajah Dowlah gave out that his chief reason for coming against Calcutta was that the English were, contrary to his orders, building new fortifications round that city.

Far, however, from adding to their fortifications, the English, to avoid giving offence to Surajah Dowlah, delayed for nearly three weeks, after hearing of his having marched, even to repair their old earthworks, which were in a ruinous state. Thus, when at last, on 7th June, they realised that their only safety lay in resisting Surajah Dowlah, there was no time to put their fortifications in any condition to be defended.

All that could be done was done. Provisions were got in, and letters were sent to Madras and to Bombay asking for help. But help from these places could not be got, for, owing to the blowing of the south-west monsoon, troops could not come by sea, and a force could not arrive by land from either place in time to be of any use.

Help was even asked from the neighbouring Dutch and French settlements. The Dutch refused to stir a finger; the French only said, "You can come and hide behind as at Chandranagore, if you like. We will send no help to Calcutta; it isn't our quarrel." Nothing remained, therefore, for the little garrison but to do the best that lay in its power.

Of the 514 men in the fort, only 174 were English. The rest were of mixed races, partly Portuguese, partly Armenian, none of them to be depended on. There were also 1500 natives, armed with old-fashioned muskets, called matchlocks, weapons, even in those days, only fit to put in a museum. In the river lay a few small lightly-armed ships.

On 16th June news of the enemy's approach was brought to Calcutta; the soldiers at once went to their posts, and all English women quitted their houses and came inside the fort. Into the fort, too, flocked 2000 Portuguese—a mob of terrified, clamouring men, women, and children, who added greatly to the difficulties of the defenders. Fighting began that afternoon, 4000 of the enemy attacking a small outlying redoubt, which stood a little way up the river from Calcutta, and which was garrisoned by fifty Englishmen, with two field-guns. That same night the officer in command of the redoubt, Ensign Pickard, led out a party of his men, drove the enemy from their position and spiked their guns, without himself losing a man.

But the English outposts were soon driven in, and gradually the whole body was forced back into the fort. Here the confusion was terrible; the Portuguese and Armenian militia were useless from fear, the lascars and others had deserted, and, in spite of much bravery shown by the English, there seemed little chance of keeping the enemy out. That night nearly all the English women were sent for safety to the small vessels which lay at anchor in the river, and at 2 a.m. a council of war was held to decide whether the whole remaining force should escape to the ships, or continue to hold the fort. But no decision was come to, and at daylight the enemy again attacked fiercely.

During the night many of the boats had deserted, and after sunrise, when an attempt was made to take the Portuguese women and children off to the ships, so great was the confusion and terror amongst them, that in the rush to get on board, the poor frantic creatures overcrowded the remaining boats so that they sank. Thus numbers perished, and many others were massacred by the enemy, who now had possession of the bank of the river above and below the fort. Now, too, Surajah Dowlah's men began to shoot fire-arrows into the vessels which lay close to the shore. So great a panic arose amongst the passengers and crews that the ships slipped their anchors and dropped three miles down the river.

Soon after this, Mr. Drake, the Governor (who up to now had behaved very well), hearing from a man that all the powder remaining in the magazines was so damp as to be unfit for use, and seeing that only two boats were left, by one of which some of his own friends were escaping, became panic-stricken and hurried into the other boat, without giving any warning to the garrison.

This was bad enough, but more remains to be told. The military commanding officer, and several others who saw the Governor embark, followed his example, and crowding also into the boat, fled, leaving the garrison to its fate. Bitter and fierce was the anger this

Chapter V: The Black Hole of Calcutta

desertion raised in the hearts of the few brave men who were left in Calcutta, and Mr. Holwell, who now took command, locked the gate leading to the river, so that at least no more might run away.

The whole garrison that remained amounted now but to 190 men. How could they, so few, hold out against the countless thousands of Surajah Dowlah!

A chance of safety still remained. One small ship had been stationed a little way up the river, and signals were now made to her to drop down abreast of the fort. When all had been done that brave men could do, the garrison had yet the hope that they might by her help save themselves. But as she came down stream, unhappily this little vessel ran aground, and remained fast on a mud-bank; and her crew, finding it impossible to get her off, left her to her fate.

And so the last hope of safety vanished. Signal after signal was made to the ships which had dropped down the river out of harm's way, but not one took any notice, not one attempted to help the doomed garrison.

During the next few hours' fighting, twenty-five of the defenders were either killed or were mortally wounded, and seventy of the others were more or less hurt. Many of the common soldiers, too, having broken open a building where arrack was stored, became hopelessly drunk, and refused to obey orders. Some of them, in their drunken folly, thinking to escape, opened one of the gates just as the enemy were about to make an assault on it, and the fort was at once rushed. Twenty of the garrison jumped over the walls, and a few struggled wearily through the river-mud till they joined the ships, but all the rest of the Englishmen were taken by Surajah Dowlah's soldiers.

At first no harm was done to the prisoners, and when Surajah Dowlah and his general, Meer Jaffier, came into the fort, the former promised Mr. Holwell, "on the word of a soldier," that he and his companions should be well treated.

But night came, the hot, stifling night, when to sleep is possible only if a punkah is without cease kept waving over the bed. On such nights, sheets and clothes seem to scorch the naked skin, and a fever of thirst consumes those who lie panting through the breathless hours. It was the season of the year when the heat in Bengal is unbearable. Night came, and Surajah Dowlah had left the fort. Orders arrived, from whom no one knows, that the prisoners should be locked up.

"Water! Water!" the poor prisoners gasped.

Chapter V: The Black Hole of Calcutta

Search was made for a suitable building in which to confine them, but none could be found.

Thereupon a native officer commanded the prisoners to go into a room, the door of which was close to where they stood. It was a very small room, a room known as the Black Hole, which had been used by the garrison as a dungeon for confining drunken soldiers. It was capable of holding three or four, or perhaps half-a-dozen men, without ill effect on those so confined.

Many of the English, knowing the size of the dungeon and its terrible want of air, (for it had but two very small windows opening on to a low-roofed verandah), objected to being put in there. Some of the prisoners laughed, thinking that the order was given merely in jest. But it was no jest.

The officer ordered his men to draw their swords, and to cut down any one who refused to enter. Thus, 146 miserable and helpless beings—145 men and one lady, a Mrs. Carey—were forced as sword's point into this small space, and the door was with difficulty closed on them. Happier their fate had they been cut down before entering.

Orme, the historian of India, whose account was written not many years after, says of this fearful time "It was the hottest season of the year and the night uncommonly sultry even at this season. The excessive pressure of their bodies against one another, and the intolerable heat which prevailed as soon as the door was shut, convinced the prisoners that it was impossible to live through the night in this horrible confinement, and violent attempts were immediately made to force the door, but without effect, for it opened inward; on which many began to give a loose to rage."

Mr. Holwell, who had been one of those fortunate enough to get near a window, tried to calm them, and he offered to a native non-commissioned officer, who stood outside near the window, a thousand rupees if he would put the prisoners into two rooms. The man said he would see what could be done, but soon he returned, saying that it was impossible. Mr. Holwell then offered him two thousand rupees, and again the man went away, whilst the unfortunate prisoners waited, hopeful, but almost fearing to be hopeful, of release. Once more the man returned, shaking his head.

"No, he said. "It is impossible. Nothing can be done. The Nawab" (Surajah Dowlah) "is asleep. Nothing can be done without his orders, and no one dares to wake him."

Now began horrors so great that one may not tell all that happened. Again the prisoners tried to break open the door, and again they failed. The heat was so unbearable that all were forced to take off their clothes; but this gave no relief. Many, overcome, sank down and rose no more. "Water! water!" the poor prisoners gasped; "for God's sake give us water!"

The non-commissioned officer who had before tried to help them, ordered some skins of water to be brought to the barred windows, but this only made matters worse.

Men fought like wild beasts to be first to cool their parched throats. They trampled on each other, and raved madly over the water that was spilled by their struggles. Those who did get water were no better off than their comrades who got none; it gave no relief, for every moment the air of the dungeon grew more and more foul, every moment the heat more great, till all but the strongest laid themselves quietly down and died.

And while this horror went on, the fiends outside, the Nawab's soldiers, crowded round the windows, holding up torches that they might lose nothing of the sight, and shrieking with laughter at the mad struggles of their victims.

Before midnight, all who were left alive, and who were not near the windows, were either unconscious or out of their minds. "Faintness," says Orme, "sometimes gave short pauses of quiet, but the first motion of any one renewed the struggle through all, under which, ever and anon, someone sunk to rise no more. At two o'clock not more than fifty remained alive."

In the morning, it was thought that Mr. Holwell's influence might still have some effect in getting the guard to open the door. But Mr. Holwell, though alive, was now unconscious. He was carried towards a window, so that the air there, being less foul, might revive him. But each man near the window refused to give up his place, for that meant possibly giving up also his life.

Only one, Captain Mills, was brave enough, unselfish enough, to give way to Mr. Howell. Hardly had the latter begun to come to his senses, when an officer, sent by Surajah Dowlah, came to inquire if the leader of the English was alive; and soon the same officer returned, and ordered the door to be opened.

Before that could be done, however, (for you will remember that the door opened inwards), it took the poor, exhausted survivors nearly half an hour before they found strength enough to clear a lane through the dead to allow the living to pass out, one by one.

Of 146 who went in, but twenty-three came out—twenty-two men, and Mrs. Carey. Happier far for her had it been if she, too, had been numbered with the dead.

A few only of those who came through that fearful night were able to make their way down the river to the ships, which still lay where they had come to an anchor. The awful tale the poor suffering creatures had to tell must surely have crushed with shame and remorse those on board who had made no effort to help them. Says Orme: "Never, perhaps, was such an opportunity of performing an heroic action so ignominiously neglected; for a single sloop, with fifteen brave men on board, might, in spite of all the efforts of the enemy, have come up, and anchoring under the fort, have carried away all who suffered in the dungeon."

It is probable that Surajah Dowlah did not mean to treat his prisoners with cruelty so fiendish. But, at the least, he never punished those who had been guilty of it, he never showed the slightest sense of pity for the sufferings of his victims, and he sent up country in chains, and cruelly ill-treated, Mr. Holwell and some of the others who, he imagined, were concealing from him the spot where, he chose to believe, the English had hidden treasure in Calcutta.

Surajah Dowlah gloried in his "victory," and he imagined that the English would never again dare to appear in arms in his country. He had wiped them out, he thought.

CHAPTER VI
THE BATTLE OF PLASSEY

News of the taking of the English factory at Cossimbazar did not reach Madras till 15th July, and the Governor at once sent a detachment of 230 European soldiers, under Major Kilpatrick, to Falta, on the river Hoogly, below Calcutta. There they arrived on 2nd August, and lay, awaiting reinforcements.

Word of the capture of Calcutta, and of the horrors of the Black Hole, came to Madras three days after Major Kilpatrick had landed at Falta, and fierce was the cry for vengeance. At once preparations were begun for the despatch of an army to punish Surajah Dowlah. To Clive was given the command of the soldiers, whilst Admiral Watson, being the senior officer, was at the head of the whole expedition.

Nine hundred good English infantry, some artillery, and 1500 well-disciplined sepoys, were soon ready, but it was not until October that the fleet could sail, and the first ship did not arrive in the Hoogly, off Falta, till 11th December. By this time most of Kilpatrick's men were on the sick list, and what with fever, and the non-arrival of one of the ships with 200 troops on board, Clive's total force was reduced to 800 Englishmen, 1200 sepoys, and a few field guns—not a very large army with which to attack a prince whose hosts might be numbered by the hundred thousand.

Meantime the Nawab, Surajah Dowlah, was "dwelling in fancied security" at Moorshedabad, his capital. In his ignorance, he had not dreamt that the despised English would dare to oppose him in his own kingdom, and it was a rude shock to the puffed-up tyrant when he received from Admiral Watson a letter saying that if payment were not at once made for the injury he had done, and redress given to those who had suffered, the Admiral would take the law into his own hands.

The Nawab at once gathered together his vast army and marched towards Calcutta. The English fleet sailed up the river till it came within ten miles of the strong fort of Budge Budge. Both Clive and

Admiral Watson saw that it would be necessary, before going farther, to take this fort. Clive wanted to sail up, then land and take it by storm, but Admiral Watson insisted that it was better to land where they were and to march up. As the Admiral was Clive's senior officer, the latter, very much against his better judgment, was obliged to give way. The troops, therefore, along with some sailors, were put on shore, and began their difficult march.

At night, tired out, they camped in two villages near the fort. But whilst they slept, the enemy fell on them, and the whole force was in great danger of becoming panic-stricken. Again Clive showed how splendid a soldier he was. Nothing could upset him or disturb his coolness. He soon rallied his men and drove back the enemy, and that same night the fort of Budge Budge was taken. A drunken sailor, pot valiant, scrambled in somehow, found that the enemy had fled, and loudly bawled to his shipmates to come and join him.

On 2nd January, Calcutta surrendered to Clive, and a few days after, he stormed and took the town of Hoogley. Surajah Dowlah with 40,000 men now advanced on Calcutta, and Clive, moving out to meet him, made as though he meant to attack, but, finding the Nawab's troops prepared, he again drew back.

A few days later, Clive, having been joined by more seamen from the fleet, marched before daylight, and in a dense fog, before any one was aware of it got right amongst the enemy. For a few moments, about six in the morning, the fog lifted, and showed Surajah Dowlah's cavalry close to him, on his flank. But the cavalry was as much taken by surprise as were Clive's men themselves, and they fled on being fired at.

Again the fog fell, and Clive had no idea in which direction to head; his men were becoming uneasy, and showed signs of panic. Things began to look very serious, for even a slight cause might now have thrown the troops into confusion, and even Clive might not have been able to pull them together again. But he never lost his coolness and presence of mind.

The fog again lifted, and Clive saw that he had got into the very centre of the enemy's camp. Any hesitation now would have been fatal. Two thousand men would have been little more than a mouthful for the 40,000 by whom they were surrounded. Boldness was the only remedy, and Clive marched on as if he had the whole world at his back. The Nawab's army broke and fled.

So great an impression did Clive's boldness make on Surajah Dowlah himself that he sent next morning a flag of truce, and agreed to grant the English everything they asked, and promised to give back all the property he had seized at Calcutta. And a few weeks later, when Clive, (hearing that war had again been declared in Europe between England and France), attacked and took the French settlement at Chandranagore, Surajah Dowlah's fear of the English became so great that he was never afterwards able to shake it off.

Clive had now done in Bengal all that he had been ordered to do. But he very well knew that if he himself were to return to Madras, Surajah Dowlah might get over his fear, and would then probably once more attack and destroy Calcutta, and this time work even greater havoc than he had done on his first visit. Therefore Clive felt that before leaving he must see the English position in Bengal made perfectly secure; and this he knew to be an impossibility so long as Surajah Dowlah ruled over the land.

Now, there were amongst the Nawab's subjects many who hated him, and who were quite ready to betray him into Clive's hands. One of these was Meer Jaffier, Surajah Dowlah's Commander-in-Chief. This man sent a message that if the English would help to make him Nawab, he would join them in turning Surajah Dowlah off the throne of Bengal. The promise was given, and many great, Indian nobles and wealthy native bankers joined Meer Daffier in his conspiracy. But in the arrangements which were then made, things arose which unhappily have left a stain on Clive's name; though he himself always held that if he had not acted as he did, everybody concerned in the conspiracy must have been murdered, and the cause of the English in India ruined.

There was amongst the conspirators a man named Omichund, a very rich merchant of Calcutta. This man was thoroughly false, and now, thinking that by his knowledge of the plot he held Clive and Meer Jaffier and all the others in, as it is called, "the hollow of his hand," that their lives were indeed at his mercy, he came to them and said that unless a bond were given to him whereby he should in the end receive twenty lakhs of rupees (two hundred thousand pounds), he would betray their secret to Surajah Dowlah. There was nothing for it, Clive thought, but to outwit the man with his own weapons, and a paper was accordingly drawn up and signed in which was promised all that Omichund asked.

Chapter VI: The Battle of Plassey

But Clive caused two documents to be written. In one, Omichund's name appeared; in the other, it did not appear. The first paper only was shown to Omichund, who went away satisfied, believing that now all was well for himself. He held a bond signed by Clive and the others, securing to himself a very large sum of money. He would now, he thought, gain more by keeping faith with Clive than he could get by betraying him. Too late, he learned how he had been duped. One man only, of all those concerned, had not signed the false document. This was Admiral Watson. Without his signature, Omichund would, of course, at once have seen that all was not as he imagined. But the Admiral refused again and again to put his name to what was a false promise. "No," he said, "I will not sign. If my name must appear, I have no objection to one of you putting it there for me, but I will not myself add my name to that document."

Accordingly, Admiral Watson's name was added by a Mr. Lusington. It was not a very moral proceeding, and long afterwards Clive's enemies made a great outcry over it. But we must remember that Clive was not acting in any way for his own benefit; it was of his country, and not of himself, that he had to think. He was, as it were, "in a cleft stick," with, so far as he could see, no other weapon at hand wherewith to counter-balance Omichund's double treachery. For the English, it meant victory or destruction. He decided that the end justified the means. He was wrong, of course, very wrong, but to the day of his death he always said that if he were again placed in alike position, he would again act as he had then done. And it is right to say that years afterwards, when Clive's enemies brought the matter to a head, the House of Commons after long discussion acquitted him of all dishonourable intent.

Surajah Dowlah, believing that he could depend on Meer Jaffier and his other nobles, now made up his mind to attack Clive, and once and for all to sweep the English out of Bengal. He had prepared a strong camp at Plassey, a village about twenty miles from his capital, Moorshedabad, and to this place he gave orders that his great army should march.

Clive at this time was at Chandranagore, where he had hurried every soldier that he could find, as well as 150 sailors whom he had borrowed from the fleet. But his whole army was very small—only 900 Englishmen, 200 men of mixed Portuguese and native blood, 2100 sepoys, and ten small guns. Few in numbers, the men were well disciplined and in good condition, and all the native regiments were officered by Englishmen. If ever you should happen to see the colours of the 1st battalion of the Dorsetshire Regiment—the old 39th—you will notice on them the word "Plassey," and the motto *"Primus in India."* The right to carry these words on their colours, that gallant 39th Regiment won under Clive at the battle of which I am now going to tell you.

With so small a force Clive marched out to meet the Nawab's host, and on 17th June the advanced guard under Major Eyre Coote took from the enemy the fort of Katwa. Here Clive learned news which caused him to think that there was more than a chance that Meer Jaffier did not mean to keep faith with the English.

Without Meer Jaffier's help the risk of defeat was too great. What was to be done? To go on seemed to promise certain destruction; to go back was little better; whilst to remain where he was meant that the natives would see that he was afraid, and would cause the conspirators to lose faith in him, possibly would turn them against him. To advance meant that he must, in the season of heavy rains, cross a deep, wide river in the face of an enemy who outnumbered him by nearly twenty to one. He was far from help; defeat would be certain death to his whole force.

For once in his life Clive hesitated, and whilst he hesitated, word came to him that Meer Jaffier had sworn to destroy the English.

A council of war was held. After discussion, Clive and twelve of his officers voted that the danger of defeat was too great if they should try to advance: they must retreat. On the other hand, seven officers, led by Major Eyre Coote, voted against this, and advised an instant attack on the Nawab's camp. By thirteen to seven the council decided not to fight.

Then Clive was left by himself. He was not happy in his mind, and as he strolled about in the shade of the trees he began to think the whole question over again. Delay, he, knew, was dangerous, and would, moreover, give time for the French to come to the help of the Nawab; the more the delay, the worse the position for the English.

In an hour Clive had made up his mind; he would fight. Going back to his quarters, he met Major Eyre Coote:

"I have changed my mind, Coote. We will advance," he said. And joyfully Eyre Coote went to make ready to cross the river.

The little army started at sunset, and after a terrible march in pouring rain, often through water waist-deep, reached Plassey at one in the morning, utterly worn out, Here they camped in a grove of mango-trees near the river, and not more than a mile from Surajah Dowlah's army. The grove was about eight hundred yards long, by three hundred broad, and round it was a ditch and a bank of earth. It was a good position to defend. Close at hand stood a little hunting-box belonging to Surajah Dowlah, and which was surrounded by a strong wall. This house Clive at once occupied.

Surajah Dowlah had in his army 35,000 infantry, who were neither well-armed nor well disciplined. But he also had no less than 15,000 good cavalry, and fifty-three guns, all of which were bigger than anything that the English could put in the field. Besides all this, the army held a very strong position, and they were helped still further by the fact that many of their guns were worked by French soldiers. The Nawab ought to have eaten Clive up.

The following morning the native army moved out of their camp and took up position, the Frenchmen with their guns being posted only 800 yards from the English. In those days, you must know, there were no such things as rifles, and it was little good, with the clumsy smooth-bore musket then in use, to fire at your enemy until you were near enough to see the whites of his eyes. Hence, artillery could then safely take up a position within half a mile of a body of infantry, which nowadays, with the modern long-distance rifle, would wipe out every gunner within five minutes. The big guns themselves in those days, carried no great distance, and they only fired round iron balls. Shells were unknown, and so infantry lying behind a mud wall were comparatively safe from danger. There was then no tempest of shrapnel-shell to burst over their heads and come scourging down into the trenches. There was no smokeless powder; a battle in those days was fought in clouds of smoke so thick that sometimes the troops went on loading and firing without, for a long time, seeing anything to fire at.

Far to Clive's right the native army stretched, almost surrounding the English position. That part nearest to the English right was commanded by Meer Jaffier. Would he keep his promise to Clive, or was he going to keep the oath he had sworn, to "destroy the English"? It was an anxious time.

The battle began at eight in the morning, and soon the Nawab's fifty-three guns were thundering, Clive's few little pop-guns making as good a reply as lay in their power. The aim of the English gunners was better than that of the enemy, but they had fewer guns, and the few they had were not heavy enough. Clive's men began to fall fast, and soon, leaving only a guard to hold the hunting-box, he withdrew them behind the shelter of the mud wall.

The enemy, thinking that this meant the beginning of the end, with yells of excitement and triumph brought their guns even closer to the mango grove and kept up a tremendous fire, to the great damage of the trees, but not of the English troops. In their excitement the Nawab's men fired too high, whilst Clive's soldiers were now making very good shooting and were causing heavy loss to the enemy. Still, at the best, the English were only holding their own, and Meer Jaffier's troops yet gave no sign of helping.

Clive himself all this time stood on the roof of the Nawab's hunting-box, whence he had a good view of the native army. As he saw column after column, regiment after regiment, gun after gun, move out and take up positions which so nearly surrounded his little force, he must have had many an anxious moment, must have doubted if this time he had not risked too much. But if he had doubts, he never showed them; then, as ever, he was perfectly cool and fearless. When such a man leads troops, when their general plays the game of war without hesitation and without hurry, men are hard to beat even when what appear to be hopeless odds are against them, and everything seems to be in the enemy's favour.

Hour after hour the thunder of the guns and the rattle of musketry went on, and neither side made much impression on the other, though men fell fast in both armies. At eleven o'clock Clive made up his mind that all he could do was to hold his present position till dark, and then, after midnight, to attack the Nawab's camp. But about midday there came on a tremendous rainstorm, such rain as is never seen in England, rain that comes lashing down in sheets that hide from view even trees a few yards away. The English quickly spread tarpaulins over their powder, and thus kept it from damage. But the Nawab's army had no tarpaulins ready, and their powder suffered so much that they could only with difficulty go on firing.

Thinking that the English must be in the same plight, and that they too would be unable to fire, one of the Nawab's generals advanced with a large body of cavalry to try to take the mango grove. But the English guns at once poured in so heavy a fire of grape—

Chapter VI: The Battle of Plassey

Clive on the roof, watching the Battle of Plassey.

which means that the cannons were loaded with clusters of small balls, instead of with the big round ones generally used—that the cavalry were sent flying back in confusion, leaving the plain strewn with dead and wounded men and horses. Amongst the dead was the general, the best man in the Nawab's army, the only one, had he known it, on whose faith he could depend. When Surajah Dowlah heard of the death of his general, his nerve quite left him. He did not entirely trust Meer Jaffier, but he sent for him, and implored him to be true. Taking off his turban, he flung it on the ground, saying: "Meer Jaffier, thou must defend that turban!' And Meer Jaffier swore that he would help his master to the end. But the treacherous dog never meant to keep faith; he at once sent word to Clive, though Clive did not receive the message till after the battle was over.

Then to the wretched Nawab came another traitor, the Rajah Dulab Ram. This man now persuaded his master to give orders to his troops to retire behind their entrenchments, and advised him to leave the field while there was yet time; the English, he said, were advancing, and the day was lost. Let his Highness the Nawab quit the field and save himself; his generals would hold the English in check and prevent their further advance.

The unhappy young Nawab, in an evil hour for himself, took this advice, and getting on a swift camel, fled to Moorshedabad, taking with him as a guard 2000 of his best cavalry, and the remainder of his army began to retire.

Clive, of course, could not know what was happening in the enemy's camp; he could not even know that the Nawab's best general was amongst the slain, and he had not got Meer Jaffier's message. He had made up his mind to hold on to the grove till night came, and then to hurl his men against the Nawab's camp. Worn out with hard work, he lay down to sleep in the hunting-box, leaving orders that he should be called if the native army showed signs of movement.

Soon Major Kilpatrick noticed that the enemy were limbering up their guns and were preparing to retire; he saw, too, that the French gunners and their guns were being left unsupported in a very dangerous position, a position from which, if the English could take it, the enemy might be fired into on their flank as they retired. Kilpatrick sent a message to Clive, and at once, with 250 Europeans and two guns, moved out from the grove to attack the French. Clive, when this message reached the hunting-box was sound asleep, and he was furious that any officer should make such a movement without asking for orders. At once he ran over to the detachment and spoke angrily to Major Kilpatrick. But at a glance he saw the extreme importance of the movement that Kilpatrick had been making, and sending that officer back for reinforcements, he himself led on the troops already on the spot. The commanding officer of the French, now seeing himself entirely deserted by the Nawab's men, poured into Clive's force one heavy discharge before retreating, and the important post he had held was seized by Clive. From this spot he advanced still further until he could fire into the Nawab's camp. This completed the confusion of the enemy.

But though confused and without a leader, the Nawab's soldiers were by no means yet beaten. They rushed out of the camp and made attack after attack on Clive, who now from two points poured in a heavy artillery fire, and from a third raked them with musketry. Charge upon charge of the Nawab's cavalry was repulsed. It was in vain that the French guns roared, and that the brave gunners worked like demons to crush the English, in vain that the native soldiers fell like corn before the scythe. It was a case of brute force against science, and science won.

Clive had noticed a large body of troops far to his right, which seemed to threaten his baggage, and he had sent a large part of his own force to hold them in check. Suddenly, as he found that no further movement was made by these troops, no attempt made by them on his baggage or his rear, he realised that they were Meer Jaffier's men. The fear of being attacked in rear thus being ended, Clive at once hurled two bodies of his troops against the new position that the French had taken up, and against a post held by the native army. The latter soon ran, and the French, finding themselves again without support, were forced to retreat, leaving their guns on the field.

The battle of Plassey was over. It only remained to damage the flying enemy as much as possible.

Clive had himself lost very few men, though he had inflicted heavy loss on the enemy. But though comparatively so few of the English were killed, this battle of Plassey, fought in June 1757, was one of the most important that ever took place in India. It really gave India to England. Long afterwards it was said by the natives that "the English Raj (or rule) would last for one hundred years after Plassey. It would end in 1857." And you know how in 1857 our rule for a time was shaken by the great Mutiny. Plassey gave to England a secure footing in Bengal, with a secure base resting on the sea (so long as she possesses a strong navy), and from that starting-point she has gradually absorbed all India. The effects of that battle have spread beyond India on all sides, as you will be able to understand later, when you are older. Then you will remember that it was Clive who won this victory of Plassey, the effects of which are felt even to this day, and which perhaps may one day affect even some of yourselves.

It was not a great "battle"; yet it was a very great "victory." It was not a great battle as far as the number of troops engaged is concerned, nor as regards the number of killed and wounded, but it was a great victory, because of its far-spreading results. And its immediate effects were very great to all concerned.

CHAPTER VII
DEATH OF SURAJAH DOWLAH—
DEFEAT OF THE DUTCH—
CLIVE'S END

Surajah Dowlah, fleeing to Moorshedabad, there learned, ere morning that his great army was totally defeated. On again in terror he fled. With his favourite wife he hurriedly embarked in a small boat on the river, in a vain attempt to find safety with the French at Bhagalpore.

That night some buildings in a deserted garden served the terror-stricken prince for a hiding-place. But he found no safety; a traitor betrayed him into the hands of Meer Jaffier, who straightway shut up in a prison the man who, till yesterday, had been his master and his friend. In the dark, soft footsteps crept stealthily to the Nawab's cell; through the thick walls came no tell-tale sound, but the pale light of dawn showed the dead face of Surajah Dowlah.

And little did Meer Jaffier (the man, you will remember, who was in command of the Nawab's army when the horrors of the Black Hole of Calcutta took place), little did he gain by his treachery to his master. He was proclaimed Subahdar, or Nawab, of Bengal, and, so far, he got his wish. But he had forever placed himself under the thumb of Clive. Nor was his conduct during and after the battle of Plassey of a kind to cause Clive ever to put any trust in him.

Meer Jaffier, besides having to confirm to the English all that Surajah Dowlah had promised them, had to grant to the East India Company all the lands lying to the south of Calcutta, together with a wider strip of ground round and outside the ditch called the Mahratta Ditch, which was then one of the defences of Calcutta. He had to give to the English all the French factories in Bengal; he had to pay enormous sums to the East India Company, and to many others. The fleet received £250,000; Mr. Drake, the Governor of Calcutta (who forsook his men, and fled to the ships when Surajah Dowlah attacked the place), received £28,000; Clive, £28,000; Major

Kilpatrick and two others £24,000 each. In addition, Clive received later a further sum of £160,000, and £175,000 was divided amongst eleven others—all this, over and above the sum of £1,000,000 paid to the East India Company. It must have cost the new Nawab something like £2,000,000, which vast sum was paid either in hard cash or in jewels.

In Clive's day in India, it was customary for both officers and men of the army and navy to receive what was called "Prize Money"—that is to say, when a town or fortress had been captured, all, the money and things of value in it were divided in certain proportions amongst the victors. It was customary also for native princes on ascending the throne to give to their supporters and friends great sums of money and rich jewels. Such practices have long been done away with, but they were the usual custom in those days.

And so Meer Jaffier's wish was gratified. But at what a cost! Nor was it only the first cost that hampered him. In order to pay the huge sums which he had promised to the English, he was obliged to tax his own people so heavily that some of the more wealthy and powerful among them rebelled. Meer Jaffier by himself was, powerless to put the rebels down; thus he was forced to come humbly to Clive, begging for help.

In this way Clive, and, through him, England, became the real master of Bengal. As the price of this help it was arranged that the East India Company should receive still further advantages.

Clive had now returned to Calcutta, where he learned that the French were making a bold attempt to overrun another part of India. Though very short of troops, without hesitation he sent Colonel Forde with 500 Englishmen, 2000 sepoys, and some guns, to oppose them. This force defeated the French time after time, and in effect secured for England the chief influence in yet another large portion of India.

Meantime Meer Jaffier was being sore pressed by a rebel prince. It became necessary for Clive himself to go to his help. But no fighting was necessary: when the English troops arrived at Patna, such was the effect of Clive's name that the rebels fled. For this help, before he again quitted Patna, Meer Jaffier gave to Clive a grant of land as a reward for his great services, or rather, he arranged that Clive, instead of himself, should henceforth receive the rent paid by the East India Company for certain lands leased to them by Meer

Chapter VII: Clive's End

Jaffier. These rents amounted to almost £30,000 per annum. Over this transaction there was, later, much ill-feeling, and Clive some time afterwards gave up to the Company his rights.

About this time trouble with the Dutch East India Company arose. The Dutch were then possessed of the rich and beautiful island of Ceylon, and, as you may remember, they also held other places in India, one of their settlements being at Chinsurah, on the Hoogly, twenty miles above Calcutta.

The Dutch were not unnaturally jealous of the position which England had made for herself in India, and especially they were angry that the English should have a monopoly of the saltpetre trade, that they should claim the right to search all ships coining up the river Hoogly, and that English pilots only should be employed on the river. They had made up their minds that an end should be put to all this, and they secretly agreed with Meer Jaffier, that if he would make ready an army to help them, they on their part would send a fleet, with large bodies of troops, to turn England out of Bengal. Of this plot Clive knew nothing.

In June 1759 the Dutch sent word to Meer Jaffier that all was ready, and in October of that year their fleet actually did arrive in the Hoogly. There were four ships, each of thirty-six guns, tow of twenty-six, and one of sixteen guns. On board, they had 700 European soldiers and 800 Malays. At Chinsurah they had 158 Europeans, besides native troops.

Against this large force Clive had but three ships of thirty guns each (none of them regular men-of-war), and one small despatch boat. His troops in Calcutta consisted only of 330 Englishmen and 1200 sepoys, and there was no chance of getting more from any other place. The position was very serious.

But it was just when things were most serious that Clive was at his best. He at once went to see Meer Jaffier, who happened then to be in Calcutta. From the Nawab's manner, it was plain to Clive that he was in the plot with the Dutch. But Clive said nothing that might cause Meer Jaffier to see that he suspected the truth; he even allowed the Nawab to leave Calcutta. Of him Clive had no great fear.

Every man in Calcutta who was fit to bear arms was now called out; the three thirty-gun ships were ordered to lie just below the fort, whilst the small despatch-boat was sent off under a press of sail to look for the English fleet, and guns were mounted in batteries which

The Duke of Dorset *fighting the Dutch fleet in the Hoogly.*

Chapter VII: Clive's End

commanded the channels in the river through which ships could sail. Just when all this preparations were made, in a lucky moment, Colonel Forde arrived with his troops, fresh from their victories over the French.

Now came a message from the Dutch, demanding that the English should give up the rights of which the Dutch complained. Clive's answer not being satisfactory to them, they at once attacked and took seven small English ships which were lying off Falta (one of them the despatch-boat which had been sent in search of the fleet); they tore down the English flag, and plundered and burnt the houses on the river-bank. The Dutch fleet then sailed up the river, and just out of reach of the English batteries, landed their troops, who were ordered to march thence to Chinsurah.

By quitting their ships the Dutch were making serious mistake, of which Clive took instant advantage. Colonel Forde was sent with his men towards Chinsurah, whilst Clive ordered Commodore Wilson, with his three ships, to attack the Dutch squadron.

Never did English sailors fight a more gallant action. Three ships, the *Duke of Dorset*, the *Calcutta*, and the *Hardwicke*, carrying in all ninety guns, attacked and defeated seven, armed with 212 guns. As soon as Wilson received his orders, he made sail.

The *Duke of Dorset*, commanded by Captain Forrester, the smallest of the three English ships, was the fastest sailer, and getting a long lead of the others, she was gallantly laid alongside the largest Dutch man-of-war. Scarcely had she got into the position when the wind changed, and the other English ships were unable to come to her help. For over half-an-hour did the little ship bravely fight the whole Dutch fleet, and when at last the wind brought up the other Englishmen, she stuck to her big enemy, and after a fight lasting two hours, took her.

Meantime the *Hardwicke* and the *Calcutta* were hammering away at the other Dutchmen, and so hot was their fire, that soon the whole Dutch fleet struck their flags, with the exception of the *Bleiswyk*, which escaped down the river, and was immediately snapped up by two other English which luckily had then just arrived. In the ship that was taken by the *Duke of Dorset*, thirty men were killed and over sixty wounded. The *Duke of Dorset* had not one man killed, though many were wounded; but she had over ninety round shot in her hull, and her rigging was cut to pieces.

One of the worst things Clive had to handle was a mutiny amongst the officers.

Chapter VII: Clive's End

Their fleet being now destroyed, the Dutch soldiers were in a most dangerous position. They must reach Chinsurah, and to reach Chinsurah they *must* defeat Colonel Forde; if they could not do so they were lost.

Meantime the commandant of the Dutch troops in Chinsurah, thinking to hamper Forde, had marched out with all his men, and had taken up a strong position at Chandranagore. But Forde with his veterans soon drove them out of their position, and took all their guns. That night he was joined by another small force of English soldiers under Captain Knox, and having got information of the whereabouts of the Dutch force which had landed from the ships, he sent a message to Clive asking for instructions, but saying that he thought he had a good chance of defeating the enemy.

Clive was playing whist when the message arrived. He did not even rise from the table when Forde's message was handed to him. After reading it, he merely penciled on the back, "Dear Forde,—Fight them immediately," sent it off, and went on with his game.

Forde did "fight them immediately," at a place called Biderra. His victory was complete. Of 700 Dutch and 800 Malays is that little army only sixty Dutch and 250 Malays escaped, and but fourteen of the former ever reached Chinsurah.

This put an end for ever to all trouble with the Dutch in India, and, moreover, the repeated victories of the English left Meer Jaffier in such a state of terror that Clive now saw that it would be safe for him to quit Bengal.

Clive was no more than thirty-five years old when he returned for the second time to England, bringing with him this time an enormous fortune. His income is said to have been as much as £40,000 a year. He was made an Irish Peer, which was less than he had desired, or expected. It did not place him in the House of Lords, but he soon obtained a seat in the House of Commons.

Like most very successful men, Clive had made during his great career in India many bitter enemies, who now set about trying to injure him. They succeeded, to a certain extent, but in the few years following Clive's departure from Bengal the state of affairs there became so threatening and so full of danger, that even his enemies had to entreat him to go out again in order to set affairs in order. He was appointed Governor-General and Commander-in-Chief of Bengal.

To understand all that Lord Clive now did, you will have to read for yourselves, when you are older, the History of India at that time.

He found Bengal a hot-bed of corruption and dishonesty; by his firm handling he purified it, and he then laid the foundations of that most splendid service, the Civil Service of India.

One of the worst and most dangerous things which Clive had at this time to handle was a mutiny in the army, a mutiny not amongst the men, but amongst the officers, who were dissatisfied over the question of pay and allowances. It was a very serious matter, but how promptly and how thoroughly Clive settled it, you must later read for yourselves; there is not room to tell of it in this little book.

One other thing which Clive did at this time may interest you. Meer Jaffier had in his will left to him a sum of £50,000. Clive did not think it right to take the money, so, instead of using it for himself, he made of it a fund for the relief of officers and men of the East India Company's Service who might be disabled by wounds or by the effects of the climate. This was called "The Lord Clive Fund," and it was in use up to the year 1858, when, on the East India Company ceasing to exist, the money came back to Clive's descendents.

Nor is there room here to tell you of the persecution of Clive by his bitter enemies in England, when, ill and sorely needing reset, he returned for the last time in 1767. His health continued to get worse; he suffered intense pain, and the incessant attacks of his enemies gave him no peace.

But he overcame all his enemies, all, save one—disease. Sleeplessness and pain were ever with him, and 1774 he ended his life.

THE END.

Lightning Source UK Ltd.
Milton Keynes UK
UKHW022029030722
405312UK00006B/650